TO A NEW HUSBAND

by Helga Sandburg

Helga Sandburg

TO A NEW HUSBAND

The World Publishing Company   New York and Cleveland

Published by The World Publishing Company
Published simultaneously in Canada
by Nelson, Foster & Scott Ltd.
First printing—1970
Library of Congress catalog card number: 79-107643
Printed in the United States of America
Design by Bob Antler

WORLD PUBLISHING
TIMES MIRROR

For the photographs, I thank: Douglas Riseborough for the jacket photo, and
the one on page 27; my daughter Paula Steichen for those on pages 20,
23, 30, 36, and 74 and one on page 58; *Medical Tribune*—Peter Hastings for
those on pages 33 and 62; Walter Halle for the one on page 48; Dwight
Boyer for one on page 58; Marianne Sandrock for one on page
58; a Cairo camel driver for the one on page 68; and lastly the master
photographer Edward Steichen for the ones on pages 44, 52, and 78.

Thanks are due also to Richard Cortland Harrison for the guitar chords that
accompany my song scores; and to my editor, Edward Kuhn, Jr.,
for his patience, enthusiasm, and hard work.

For my uncle Edward Steichen with love

CONTENTS

Helga Sandburg
Cleveland, Ohio
Summer, 1969

ALL of my books, as with most fiction writers, are autobiographical. They carry seeds of happenings of my life and parts, at least, of persons and the creatures and the countryside close to me in the past or now. Some of them are frankly history, dealing with my earliest memories of the tall vague figure, the poet and singer of my childhood household, who lifted me to walk the ceilings of all the rooms of our home; until my days as a single girl, after two divorces and a daughter and son, in a flat in Washington, D.C., from which I sallied out to lecture for a New York bureau two or three times a month; and where, my children grown, pressed by necessity, I began to write with greater diligence.

Poems are written in celebration of events and feelings. In my first collection of poetry, *The Unicorns,* they ranged from one written on my grandfather's death a quarter of a century before, to new ones I was composing for the man I was deciding to marry and to whom I would dedicate the book. The poems in this present collection are intimate, personal, and have to do with recent years. In common with most poets, it is my hope that in some way they are the voice of those who read them.

FOREWORD

IT was during my early forties that divorce happened. Subsequently, I led a vigorous life as a writer, one of its happier aspects being that I found at last I had time. During the uninterrupted long hours, which often merged into the dark, while my friends assumed that I was dancing the gay nights away, as might have seemed justifiable, I could apply myself in my slow fashion to my work, not answering the telephone or doorbell, content. My love affairs, in this country and abroad, whether protracted or brief, were a delight since, unlike marriage, one had some control over the life of each. I felt a strong hesitancy about ever reentering the bonds of wedlock.

When I traveled in Europe for the State Department during my first days as a bachelor girl, I bought a guitar in Göteborg, Sweden. On return to my flat in Washington, D.C., I mastered the chords well enough to accompany myself at songs I had learned from my father throughout my childhood: "Abdul, the Bulbul Ameer," "The Spanish Cavalier," various prison, railroad, pioneer, mountain, or sailor songs. The guitar fulfilled a certain need in me and often when I picked it up in the quiet late night, promising myself to spend fifteen minutes with it before returning, disciplined, to my desk, I would find that hours had passed while I went through one after another of old family favorites. I was satisfied with my new life.

DIVORCE

Phoenix

Before the separation
When the veins of our hands lay often together
And our mouths were understanding
Love-poetry came easy

After our angry voices
I stayed myself from writing
I left arranging of words
Empty windows and dusty doors
Were my world

Now that I have found again the easy sky
And have given up the cough drops
And spring is replacing the cobwebs
That had stretched

I will write another love poem
And give it to
Anyone who passes

Dover Beach the Second

Once-love, you were not true : mark that.
It is the way I say ; you were not.
If only for my loss there were a frightful cause to blame ;
If, standing at the window, I could have quivering claimed,
"Fierce warring men are approaching the town gate.
You must from me run !" Alas, no, reprobate,
It was only that in your house, then mine, into white gleam
Of kitchen you'd disappear again and once again,
Emerging momentarily assuaged with plates of meat
Or bowls of things, savory, odorous, to you important.
I put up with it because you said it was marriage,
But sly-eyed, Xanthippe, the while your measure I gauged.
It was clear, the wound between you and me,
Which gaped ever wider while you forgot my beauty !

I tell it now plain ; you were not true.
And for this, hateless, I had at last to go
And make a room of my own where in dark gentle pain
I might build my dignity again. I am a proud woman
(Made as women believe for great love ; the very least
Of us, cheated in her man, is convinced
Of that !) But then, there is so much, so much, yes ?
Besides spouse and house, so one day one is able, no less,
To stumble suddenly up from table and confess, "Chéri,
Ta-ta. It's over the river, Socrates. You've seen the last of me !"

Miss S

The rather well-meaning Mrs. G
Through no mortal fault that she can see
Is presently Miss S and free,
Deposed from the wifely throne.

With gentle reluctance she will own
The pleasures of her new bachelordom:
The hot bath at midnight, breakfast at sun,
No reports, written or oral, to make.

When friends say to her, now for heaven's sake,
Marry again, her head she'll shake.
She won't even talk for the talking's sake,
And she's given up cockatiel, dog and cat,

That she used to fondle upon a lap
While talking with husband of this and that,
Of an inconsequential which or what.
She strums her guitar, she will confess,

With enthusiasm that's limitless.
She travels by streetcar — *The Shoppers' Express,*
And is found to be punctual less and less,
The rather well-meaning Miss S!

The Hour Was

I have been loved. "Erat hora," a poet said long ago.
Giving up my identity in time's backwash,
Surrounded by the undertow, I returned to the beginning,
To pre-Christian religious civilized flesh;
Being honey in the darkness of the hot hollow tree,
Pillaged by a bruin crow-haired as midnight's sea,
With eyes like an amber-hued locust-bloom-fed bee.

I have been loved. "Erat hora." And when he and I are dust,
Felled by the wheeling of the brave enormous stars
Still will be heard the echo of our precious lust,
And still will be on the air the delicate scenting such as sheds
From anemones, juicy-stemmed and black-hearted and unchaste,
Passion-pictures of carmine and lavender which fade in haste.

Others more fair or clever perhaps than I or lover
And singing sweeter songs than this one ever,
May succeed sometime our hour to out-distance;
Time's not gauged by clock hands but by a deed's significance.

The Visit

Come in, if you will, but then leave soon.
Close the door quietly after you, please.
Don't break the silence of my rooms. I would keep
The feeling I have deep in me of trees
And grassy unconstricted places. I have been
To see my lover. It clings to me,
The luster. Tonight the faces of the stars
Will burn two degrees brighter because of it.

Don't speak, please, for I smell the breath
Of that blue-flowered weed you find sometimes
Growing tight in breasts of certain fields,
That is, if you kneel and search for it. Come in,
But go soon. Great fabled kine are lying down
In groups by woods, and rain anoints their hides,
Scented, silken. Hush! I am yet struck dumb
By that rareness from which I have lately come.

Three Men in Stockholm
(Dawn, May 1961 – to U. S.)

I have walked up a ramp of old unwarmed stone
(Having left you and your blue eyes an hour ago)
And seen an iron beast in the town of Stockholm,
On whose back sits George holy hero;
Before kneels the maiden in her pious swound
While under the hooves the amoral dragon
           continually takes his wound.

I have passed a metal man on the grass with a sword
Unsheathed in one of his gauntleted hands; spiked chains
Encircle him (you stroked your yellow beard
Slowly with a heavy thumb); Karl the Twelfth seems
To dance the minuet as he points at the sky
To the dawn in the east and speaks in words of stone
           of justice and arms and equality.

I have come to the Reisen Hotel and from the sun-pale window
Watched on the strand some gentled white leviathan
Approach bawling to be leashed to the wharf (tomorrow
You say you must go to France); all the flags sigh, "Sweden,"
In the colors strung from the ships' masts,
Matching blond saints and lady-faced kings
           and anguished pierced blue-eyed beasts.

(How can you, having just come to me, go away so soon?
You who are in all your strange strong ways—Sweden)

Letter

Just now when the wind blew
Across me standing here in the
Doorway of my house I remembered
Last night in some small hour of the
Morning I woke from a bad dream and
Lay there in the dark afraid not
Knowing why I woke or why afraid I
Thought the lonely dark is my sarcophagus
There is no sound the world is dead and
I am alone here and empty I thought of
The love between us how you lay in
Another land sleeping away from me there
Is no sound my mouth is cotton
My limbs are no part of me
I wonder what made me wake.

Are you well?

Goodbye, Darling, It Was Great Fun

We parted at the station and he turned to me;
The whistle started blowing, he got ready to run;
He kissed me on the cheek rather hastily
And said, "Goodbye, darling, it was great fun!

"Goodbye, darling, it was great fun,
It was such fun, but I've got to run;
I'll call you from Chicago or from New Orleans,
I'll send you a postcard from Washington!"

First I got an airmail from Penobscot Bay;
Then it was a letter stamped at Willow Run;
And each of them was ended in the same old way,
Saying, "Goodbye, darling, it was great fun!"

Goodbye, Darling, It Was Great Fun

L'Affaire Est Morte; Vive l'Affaire!

You said that you would always be faithful
And you never would pass the brink,
Then, darling, why were cigarettes in your bedroom
And dishes for two in your sink?
L'affaire est morte; vive l'affaire!

They told me, "She's a flame from his past, my dear,
And she never will let him go."
I asked you and you said, "No, never, my sweet,
I never see her. Never. No!
L'affaire est morte; vive l'affaire.

"Except maybe now and then occasionally,
Since I've known her for so many a year.
She's an old old ember dying slowly
And I'm letting her down easy, my dear.
L'affaire est morte; vive l'affaire."

They told me, "There's another in Chicago, too."
I said, "Darlings, that never can be,
For he only flies out there on business
And business is picking up lately."
L'affaire est morte; vive l'affaire.

You said, "My sweet, I can't see you this evening.
My work is piled up; it's just a shame."
I phoned and it wasn't you answered
And I asked, "Are you the new flame?"
L'affaire est morte; vive l'affaire.

You said, "Love, I can't see you in the next ten days,
For business is calling me again."
But when you came back from Chicago,
You had a Puerto Rican tan!
L'affaire est morte; vive l'affaire.

Now, my friend, I don't mind your wandering;
And I don't care how many broads you've made,
But will you please stop saying "sister" and "cousin"
And call a spade a spade!
L'affaire est morte; vive l'affaire!

L'Affaire Est Morte; Vive l'Affaire!

[After "Frankie and Johnny"]

Yours Very Sincerely, George Crile

I waited to hear, all anxious to know
The news—I wanted your style,
But when your letter came in the mail,
It said, "Yours very sincerely, George Crile."

I thought that something ought to be done,
I wrote, I protested, meanwhile
On my doorstep was another love note
Signed, "Yours very sincerely, George Crile."

(I wonder what he's doing just now,
I'll bet his out-going mail's in a pile,
And I'm not so sure each letter ends like mine:
"Yours very sincerely, George Crile!")

Yours Very Sincerely, George Crile

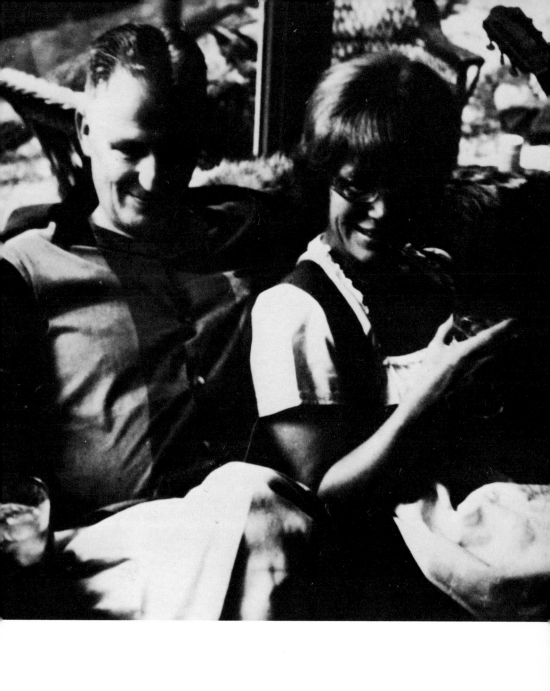

AS I was leaving my Washington bachelor flat, known as the "Bit of Paradise," I dedicated *The Unicorns* to George Crile (Barney). The last poem explained our inevitable marriage:

> *Love, you said, is of its own self wove,*
> *It is not us; there is no act to prove.*
> *In its green time this thing will choose to move,*
> *And then into the dream stood love.*

We visited my family on their farm in Flat Rock, North Carolina, and my father, in his eighties, looked Barney up and down, argued with him on the state of the nation, and said that if we were in love, as captain of the household, he'd be happy to perform the wedding. We felt that after his benediction, a visit to a civil official was uncalled for. However, one of Barney's daughters burst into tears at the news, declaring that the community would be scandalized, and so we took out a license and in the office of a Justice of the Peace in our nation's capital, an imposing Negro in purple robes spoke the legal words.

My new home was in Cleveland. Barney had been a widower for less than a year. A surgeon by profession, and a writer, he was also an amateur naturalist. His back yard was a fenced-in garden where a white swan lived, some mallards and wood ducks nested, and a few guinea pigs and a brown hare ran loose. Out in the country was a two-hundred-acre rambling place where run-down buildings stood, which had once belonged to Barney's father. We spent occasional weekends there and built a small house and more ponds for the varied wildfowl.

In the first spring, Barney gave me a White Fallow fawn, who stayed in the kitchen and the garden of the town house. In the evenings, I would play my guitar out in the garden, singing old ballads as well as tunes of my own. He would join in sometimes, his words often varying from mine. But he seemed most pleased to sit back in the sunset, half-listening, the smoke of his cigar gray and fragrant, watching the deer moving among the other twilight-feeding creatures. My life had come full circle and I was content.

REMARRIAGE

The Forming of Our Love

Do you recall the forming of our love
When you and I went hunting that first time
As dawn was making up its mind to be
And following on a thousand blackbirds' wings
Came a dozen yelping wild geese in a string?
I saw your arms come up but held my tongue.

The great lead gander dipped and swung
Down into the field and shrieking gun;
I watched his spiraled feathers as he fell
Angelic through the air and heard his thud.
Both of us went running to his side
To kneel bemused above him as he died.

I sobbed upon his blood and dark sweet eye;
I looked at you and you were weeping too.
"I don't know why I didn't speak!" I cried.
"I've shot my last wild goose. It's true,
Like you I will prefer them quick not dead.
Don't leave me, love, because of this," you said.

Letter to a New Husband

Stranger, to your house I came two moons ago,
Where great bird stands erect on clumsy feet
Outside our door and pecks upon the pane
To tell me something I don't understand.
His beak opens to take the bread I proffer;
Bending his long neck, his eye meets mine.

He is recalling other hands and eyes;
I know no other swan. In the mirrors of our house
Tremble faces now and then, shadowless ghosts,
Whose gaze I meet with love I manufacture out of need.
Moths flutter from old rugs and skins brought down
From attic rooms and holding cocoons
Spun in another time. Nothing remains the same.
If your dreams are invaded by wandering presences
Who are gentle and place the keys and turn the locks,
Are you learning, like me, to welcome them where they belong?

Husband, light the lamps and take me to your arms.
In the dawnlight the swan walks to the door,
His neck upstretched, impatient his call.
The wind through the winter window smells of spring.
Let tomorrow come. I sit before the mirror
And run the comb through my hair and wait upon your return.

Anniversary Anagram

Barney, tonight in the garden there is no sound
All the moon-addled animals are rooted to the ground
Roses and geraniums and frogs are closing their eyes
Not even the waterfall is falling—in surprise
Enchantment is the name of this place you gave to me
Your garden is aware of our anniversary.

Come into this shadowed place which is my amulet
Realize it is but a year since we met
In your arms I'll praise how I'm your debtor
Love, I cannot seem to say this better
Either in a letter or your garden spellbound.

When I Lay in the Darkness

When I lay in the darkness by your side
Last night, husband, I woke terrified,
Because of a dream in which I died
In another life in a yesterday somewhere.

I felt your breathing move upon the room
And repented of all action still undone,
Was ashamed of every word unspoken,
Melancholy, appalled, in the dark.

Husband, dreams are dreamed so we may see
The instant and its spare reality.
You stirred and your arms enclosed me
And time was all the time it ever was.

34

I Lie Between Sun-Scented Sheets

I lie between sun-scented sheets, husband,
And dwell upon your goodness.
The light about us is that of the dawn,
And shapes within the room just clothed in dark
Begin to make a dresser and a chair
As well as your face breathing there.
The dawnlight has a unique quality
That sets it apart from the rest of day;
Slow is the light, flesh glows, and no color is.

Instead of knowing as I sometimes do
That I hold you too closely in my love
I wish that I might be some old-time wife
Living in a pagan springtime town,
Who would contrive an endless festival
To celebrate the goodness that is you.
I would have music like the moon and planets make,
Then have some Michelangelo your portrait paint
Across the sky itself that all might see!

Réalité

Husband, you are master of this place and three years ago
Took me for its mistress. *I am trying to tell you something.*
I have been swimming naked in the cold pond's water
And lie now on the gray warmed boards of the pier.

A wood duck preens herself on the wornout raft,
A dragonfly hovers and settles by my hand,
A frog honks twice and is still.
The duck drops into the water and floats nearby,
The cool wind rushes through the locusts and oaks.
Ripples glisten across the green-dark water,
Sticks snap and rustle in the bordering woods,
The sky is indigo with no hint of cloud.
Look, I am trying to tell you something.

The pale water lilies silently spread their blooms
By ragged polished posts of another time,
The mallow pinkly glows on the bank above its mirrored self.
The knotholes on the pier boards about me are telling time,
As are the spikeheads rusting, the cobwebs gleaming.
The frog is honking again, the dragonfly is leaving.

Rising, I hear the sighs from the darkened woods
And gazing out, meet the glittering eyes
Of ancient promiscuous wandering deities.
Look, I am trying to say that your eyes are a brilliant blue
And that your voice is tender-timbred to me,
There is a scar on your left hand telling time,
And no matter where I am you are with me.

The Middle of Time

Something is happening in the kitchen there
It is not yet time for the guests to come
The woman is standing beside the dining table
He is upstairs and the quarrel has stopped ringing
Through all the house's rooms and she is beholding
What the twilight which has just struck is doing

The red wine in the vinhaber is blazing darkly
The unused polished glasses and silver glinting
The blue plates which will soon be black are burning
She cannot speak resting her hand upon a chair
Which is in ancient Greece or Persia or Rome
Or one in some far-fetched future room of the moon

The woman is stalled there in the middle of time
Which is holding still at her twilighted table
Outside the golden evening is beginning to be night
All colors not yet so soon will be colorless
The grass is glowing below the elm which gathers
Its leaves for a final burst of green radiance

The woman does not want the vinhaber emptied
The candles lit or the gay guests ever to arrive
Her chic dress to be passé or her emerald lost
Gift of the smoldering husband descending the stairs
Pushing the door to and coming into her arms
But their kiss is marking the ending of the twilight

Lo, Out Upon the Blue Lake

Lo, out upon the blue lake every wave holds still;
The brightly-colored bathers lie unmoving in the noon;
I am thinking that in all ways I am to you faithful,
Unstirred by the burning water and the sun,
Letting the book slip from my hand,
Dwelling on the ageless distant scene and sky;
I deemed once only to read of great love, husband,
And to deserve but not experience the rarity.

Lo, the waves are moving now upon the brilliant sea,
And the bathers stir among each other in their mortality.

Mirrors

I

Talking to Mother by long distance telephone,
Her voice snaps, sharp and clear at eighty-five,
"I can tell you, it's always a surprise
When I look into a mirror nowadays.
I don't think of myself as being that way!"

II

In our house are only old mirrors,
Some sadly in want of silvering and repair,
I'll have no unused virginal mirrors,
Hanging inexperienced anywhere.
The mirrors of our house won't let me go;
Family secrets confounded in them lie;
It is said that if a robber shoots a mirror
The ghosts within it gasp and groan and die.
Standing before the mirror in the bedroom,
Seeing the me that others do not see
(For here the left is right and right is left),
Past passers-by constantly throng near me.
Here are the phantom shapes of former wives,
Strong men, shadowy shades of other days,
Here the scandalous workmen found the wine
And toast themselves while the scaffold sways.
Dashing, the dogs come in to rear and stare
At softly-growling selves who have no scent.
Delighted, the housemaid hugs the hired man
Who gave her the lottery number which paid her rent.

Here came one this morning to comb his hair,
In the chronicling glass to stand and knot his tie,
His eyes went wandering to the mirror's white bed
And found me there in the mirror's country.

Old mirrors, your historical ways I praise,
And I'll never have a new one all my days.

III

I am the truth,
Inasmuch as that is possible;
Small children and dogs adore me,
Manly men ignore me,
Women continually explore me.

I am accurate,
Inasmuch as it is possible;
Within my silver glass
The lovely lass in time must pass,
The aged lady cries "Alas!"

IV

If candles glow upon the dining table
And mirrors hang upon opposing walls
And you and I, husband, are repeated
Along with candles, glasses, and with flowers,
Does the diminishing scene contain parents
And theirs and theirs unto the primitive tree?
Or are those children of ours and their children
Reversing direction to endless eternity?
Mirrors, mirrors, by our table,
Fairy tale, allegory, parable, and fable!

Anniversary Anagram II

Beloved, it is six years since we met;
A day it might be or a century;
Religious, I have dropped all bargaining;
Nor heaven nor hell can threaten or tempt me;
Everyone has a treasure to be taken;
You but increased my store of harmony.

Clearly, you could have torn my angel down,
Righteous with scientific anarchy;
I'd not have argued with a non-believing mind.
Love, your reality illuminates my days;
Each evening we meet is an anniversary!

IN all families are the strong and weak, the old and young, death and life. In mine, three individuals were particularly strong—my mother and father, Paula and Carl Sandburg, and my mother's brother, Edward Steichen. Their vitality, camaraderie, and courage made a strong impression on me as I grew up. I felt their immortality. Then my father, of whom my mother said lately, "There are some men who should never die and Carl is one of those," died. His great-grandson was at the funeral, still in his mother's womb. Now Steichen, hale at ninety, has celebrated another birthday, and my mother, in her late eighties, said to Barney and me, "I just wish I looked as good as I feel!"

Thinking of my grandchild Sascha, the message of immortality remains strong.

THE FAMILY

Poems for a Father, I

I remember you in various ways;
The picture I have of you of those days
Differs perhaps from what you'd think it is.
Living is an unprobed game that children play
Since everyone else is doing it too.
You sat on the house's top above three stairways,
Your skin caging the sun with brassed felicity,
And spoke to me father's counsel to which I gave little mind,
Though admiring your glad attitude and being
Sure that the world was firm, since you held
Its reins so exceeding well. The smoke
Had gone from your cold clenched cigar; the wood
Of the orange crate was hot to touch; in back
Of you the iron grill was flooded by a trumpet vine;
The tropical blooms hid clustering from
The sun which was stamped with your name,
Which belonged I knew to you.
That was one thing, the sun; another was
Your voice humming as you descended uncounted stairs
To where the rest of us were at table.
Two mad beautiful Irish setters howling joy
Prefaced your arrival. A song had begun lusty
When you reached the second staircase; it might be,
"Everybody works at our house but my old man!"
The faces in the room went wheeling to your voice. Then
Your affection for night, your walking through it,
Into its blackness where occasionally glowed
One evening star like a tiny sun
Or the beginning moon like a cobweb looped
Or an old sated one in a blue blaze.
For these thanks: the globe and bugle blooms, the red dogs
And song, and the night which I hold on temporary loan.

45

Conversations Overheard;
Mother and Uncle, Daughter and Son

Listen a while; the old ones are talking—brother and sister.
Listen a while. "Remember? It's a long way from those days.
Remember that one-and-a-half storey cottage?"
"And the thirty-foot front? And the cow pasture nearby?"
"It's a long long way we've come." "Long, all of us on fire."
The hammock swings in the sun in the morning
On the lawn. They speak of their mother's death: *she.*
"Is that pillow in the right place?"
The sister stands at the hammock, her white hair shines
In the gleam; the curls have escaped the bun.
"At the very last I saw recognition in her eyes."
"*She* knew me! I'm sure of it." "As *she* was slipping away.
Yes." Ravished, the brother calls it back, an old sorrow.
"And once I went to see the grove of trees and the pond I knew
As a little boy. There was only a puddle
And a bush, no more; I am certain of the spot."
Listen a while; the voices like pigeons, retelling.
"Remember? Remember?" "A long way. Long."

Listen a while; the children are talking—brother and sister.
Listen a while. Stand behind the door in the noon heat to hear.
"Some day I'll have my own house and my own way. I will
Some day." "I'll set this world on fire."
The sister stands beside the cot with wounded eyes.
"In this country are fifty million poor. I'll not have children."
"I'll have six." But her chin is small and shapely and quivers
With her indignation. "Some day someone's got to change that."
Listen a while; like doves in a cote, persistent.
The brother lies stretched and staring, like a knight
Graven upon a sarcophagus in a French cathedral.
"Some day. You'll see." "Some day before long."

Sonnet About My Daughter Among the Flowers

Paula comes before them, sprinkling can in hand,
Trailing a hose, and all the petals start to turn,
Until the blooms are gazing where she stands,
Moody-faced, blue-jean clad, freckled, burned.

Paula somehow knows the feeling in their toes
For dampness now or dryness then, the urgent need
For long unhurried sleep; somehow she knows.
The little or great potential of each seed.

She hovers above the green growing things for hours,
Abstracted, surprised, stirred—Paula among the flowers.

Daughter-in-Law, I Praise You
(FOR ELISABETH STEININGER STEICHEN)

Daughter-in-law, I praise you for your power.
Before you finally got your trunks and visa together
So you could come and join him over here,
My son roamed the house like a leashed tiger.

Helpless with the weight of his new burden,
His eyes burned with a dark uneasy fire.
I'd thought sometimes that he might find quickly a wife,
But never that he could change because of her.

He wrote *I love you* on a hundred tiny slips of paper
And shoved them all into an envelope clumsily;
"I've told her to put them by her mirror and toothbrush,
In her purse and shoes, beside her plate at tea."

And then you came, beautiful, and stood in his arm;
His somber nature changed under your gaiety;
Because you've made him so he now laughs that way,
Daughter-in-law, I praise you constantly!

Poems for a Father, II

When my father decided not to die after all,
My mother asked the hired man to shave his beard.
He sat up nobly in his bed and made no protest,
Amenable to her vanity, her fears allayed.

Father, you were beautiful, your brain on fire!
You lay at eighty-seven on the high white bed,
Bearded, brilliant-eyed, your mind intent upon itself.
Father, lying there you seemed so young.

And I your senior, still the obedient child,
Quelled by the blaze when your eye fell on me,
Hoping, helpless, that I'd been recognized
And not thought some sister or cousin or aunt.

Now, Father, you are going to live yet a while;
You used to prophesy your end would come
When you reached an age divisible by eleven;
We should have remembered and believed and not doubted.

Father, take your time leaving this life;
Go slowly, not for your, but for our sake!

Poems for a Father, III

Father, once you said that in the grace of God you might,
As did Hokusai, live to the age of eighty-nine;
I thought my own thoughts about the prophecy:
Take your time leaving this life,
Go slowly, not for your, but for our sake.

Father, when you went away finally
The striped lily, waiting to bloom, bloomed,
Taking up your going breath,
Standing among other-colored lilies and crimson dahlias
In the old garden's morning fog.

I was not there, but the others told me
Of your favorite nurse, the beautiful Negro, Mrs. Green,
Putting Chopin on the record player a few evenings before
And bringing you a *Magnolia Grandiflora* flower,
White-petaled and a foot across, as was her custom
From the great tree outside your balcony,
And how you were sleeping and night began coming on
And how the room became like a cup brimming over
With that music and the heavy lemon scent of the enormous flower
And how everyone then somehow felt better
And more able to endure your inevitable leaving.

Father, when they told me to come I could not weep
And arrived serious and went to look at your room,
Where the magnolia bloom, now brown and sculptured,
Still was upon the white mantel near where the high bed,
Now removed along with the wheelchair, had been.
When I had helped to carry the trays away,
That held the bottles and spoons and glasses and pills
And threw them all somewhere and changed the room
So chairs and lamps and tables were patterned anew,

And fresh dahlias and zinnias and lilies were brought in
From the gardens of my mother which hem the house,
I said, "I am going to look at him," and went.

Father, you wore the suit they had picked with care,
One of your old double-breasted ones, the tie broad
And red and black, and your hands resting quiet, familiar,
And your face not you, but your shell, so I let you go
For the first time and went unweeping into the sun.
Flowers and relations kept coming into the house:
Chrysanthemums and carnations and arranged red roses,
The bearded brother of my mother, son, daughter-in-law, daughter,
Alien never-seen cousins and aunts, children become adults,
Placed helter skelter about the house's rooms,
Settling themselves here and there, pulling from pockets
Photographs and notebooks implicating you with their lives.

Father, it was a celebration and everyone laughed
And kept watching my mother to see if she stayed strong,
Which would make them so.
The table's three unused leaves were brought from the cellar
And the long yellow damask cloth unfolded.
Chairs and plates were placed for most of us,
Some overflowing into window seats.
A roasted rare beef was sliced and a chocolate cake,
Creamy yellow iced which some neighbor had sent.
My bearded uncle, who loves flowers the way my mother does
Declared that he had dug and pirated roots
From her old garden to take back with him,
Not knowing they came from the same striped lily
Which had bloomed in recognition of you.
My mother remembered that when you came in towns to lecture
You went to libraries to find how many books were stolen
Of yours, pleased when the number exceeded other authors.
And still outside the sun was blazing on the pines
And someone was sitting in your chair at the table's head.

54

The breeze and the yellow ball above behaved,
The green trees' needles became inordinately green,
And no rain dared to rain,
As the family and invited nurses and maids
Stood on your white porch waiting to be told to go,
Pulling on gloves and relating what you said to them and when,
And Mrs. Green asked to see your rooms
Where the position of everything was now changed.

The cars were driving down your driveway,
Myself in the second one, recollecting other days
When we broke speed limits making trains and planes.
The car ahead which held my mother and sister and uncle
Halted, and he clambered out, cane in hand,
And went to break a green pine branch for love.
And the white police car with the red flashing on its roof
Was guiding us to where your shell would come.

Father, the row of candles on each of the candelabra wavered,
Burning down thinly beyond the altar,
To which your closed coffin lay perpendicular,
Your feet toward it within your pale satin bed.
My uncle placed his green branch over your head,
And I gazed upon the church's pearl-colored pall
While the minister read words from your books
And, for the second time, now weeping, I let you go.

That night most of the relatives went away,
The flowers in your rooms were growing old,
Alone I held your worn guitar and sang your songs
And wondered if you'd gone now from our lives.
Then all at once I heard from another room
My children's and my mother's voices laugh.
I felt the essence of yourself in them
And thank you for the way you chose to go.

Song for Sascha

I can't talk much with my grandson
He's eight hundred miles away
But I hear from his mother and father
That he said three words today

He put his socks in the fishbowl
And strawberry jam in his shoe
And the three words on his first birthday
Were *Mama* and *Teddy* and *Poo*

When Sascha and I met six months ago
And he laughed his belly laugh
I thought I'd love my grandson
Till the cow turned into a calf

Till the moon became a pumpkin
And butterflies changed into birds
And yesterday was tomorrow
And whistles were used for words

Till trees get up and dance around
And daisies begin to sing
And the North Star runs away to the south
And nothing is everything

Till questions turn into answers
And a coat becomes a hat
I'll still be loving Sascha
And nothing will ever change that

I was reared in the sand dune country of Lake Michigan and have lived on farms much of my life, taking my living from the soil and the creatures I cared for. During my days in the Washington flat, most of my writing was concerned with memories of the land. My hands are broad and strong; one of my Swedish friends has said that I resemble the farm girls of Östergötland.

Barney and I spend three or four days a week in the country now, living in the one-room house, with its small adjoining barn, which we built on our piece of woods and pasture where Barney had roamed as a child. There we keep our fallow deer, capybaras, peafowl, crows, vultures, and various other animals and birds, and also foster the natural wildlife.

Barney and I approach our creatures in different ways. His is that of a biologist, observing the behavior of the species, sometimes not even knowing the personal name which I have given each. On the other hand, I have cherished our squirrels, Huntington and Richard, for their own idiosyncrasies, which differ as much as those of any of my human friends. And our crows, Smokey Joe and William Bailey, the former aggressive, the latter shy, had individual and distinct personalities that were clear to me. If it is true with mankind that the uniqueness of the individual is the chief quality essential to a soul, then I recognize the existence of the same quality in my various birds and beasts.

THE
COUNTRY

Location of Things Song

[After folk tune]

58

Location of Things Song

The lamb is in the library
And the rabbit's in her pen,
The crow is chasing sparrows,
Then where's the speckled hen?

The hen is in the kitchen now,
And the guinea pig's running free,
The squirrel is in the finches' cage,
Then where can Gustav be?

Gustav's in the living room,
Sleeping with the goose,
Then where's the capybara?
Who could have turned her loose?

The mallards are on the wood duck pond
And so is the big white swan,
The fawn is in the upstairs hall,
Then where has the turkey gone?

He's pecking at the window pane,
While his wife's up in the tree,
Roosting with the pheasants,
Then where can the pigeon be?

The pigeon's in the peacock's house
And the dove has flown somewhere,
But Helga's sitting in the lap
Of Barney in his chair.

Ode to a Guinea Pig
Less Than One Day Old

Last night the guinea pig who lives
    in our kitchen
Gave birth to three, as beautiful as she,
    young!
I have the smallest in my palm,
Who surveys me, remains calm
And attends to my guinea pig psalm:

Oh little beast, oh mystery!
Smooth of coat and bright of eye,
Seventy days in the womb you lay
And then sprang forth so splendidly
And fearless about the world began to roam!

This is no poem, but an encomium.

Eulogy for a Crow

Judging by larger graver sorrows,
The loss to some may seem a paltry one,
But this morning when I opened my country door
My crow, William, lay like a small black stone,
Pierced by the horned owl's claw to the bone.

Needless death is a thing I ponder on,
For the owl by the death of William made no gain.
Is the lesson of the going of my cheerful bird
That one must learn by small to bear large pain
And so stand the deaths of all innocent men?

William, missed on my walks today and tomorrow,
Swift, light-bodied, talkative—small sorrow!

60

Poems to the Dog, Gustav

I

Look, the dog's name is Gustav,
And his eyes are golden; he is huge,
Shaggy-coated and mustached,
Gray-bearded and beetle-browed.

Look, he is noble and responsible;
If I move about the house in the small hours,
His dark padding follows me;
Weary, he cannot lie and dream upstairs.

Look, he does not bore me with discussions,
He does not insist that I listen,
He does not mind whether I weep or shout.
I call the dog, Gustav, marvelous!

II

Little there is in me that comprehends
The riddle of this dog's devotion;
Ravished with love, he comes to gaze at me,
Enchanted if I turn to look at him.

When I pack my bags to make a trip,
He goes at once to sulk at top of stair;
If I rush to weep upon my bed,
He follows me to sigh and settle there.

Man has worn his gods out one by one,
Busy with his own destruction,
But golden-eyed Gustav has only to nudge my hand
And paradise is there at his command!

The Yearling

The deer that we took from her mother in the spring
And put in our back yard has changed,
And where she once moved hesitant and small
Through towering iris clumps and lily stems,
She now goes arrogant across the snow
And intends to paw the grass up where she will.
The dog that she once viewed as dangerous
Comes to help her ravage our poor lawn;
He sniffs at her and in a graceful way
She rears on her hind legs and strikes him with her fore,
Leaps into the air and bounds and runs.
Our deer is delighted to be grown!

The Killer

Oh, blood on the snow and the circling tracks
And the carcass of the hamstrung young buck deer!
The bare frozen trees with their unborn flowers laden
All were witness to the moonlight-dancing farmer's dog.
The icy floor beneath is the roof to the bedrooms
Of all the underground creatures who heard it happen,
The stomping tranced deer falling under the growls
Of the one who hangs his head now, licking the farmer's hand.
Insects in their winter shrouds are refusing to move,
The snow is hurrying to cover the murder over,
Falling forever from the darkening March skies.
Oh, some say there will not even be a spring this year!

Three Serpents in a Well in a Field

Yesterday in the hot field behind our house,
We came upon a drying well of some other year
All grown over with crowding clover.
We pulled away the rusty iron cover
And gazed down into the gloom.

Oh mystery! Oh beautiful! Oh terror!
Three reptiles common to our countryside,
Yellow Rat Snakes, harmless constrictors,
Coiled about the ancient roped bucket
And gazed up blindly from the gloom.

Oh trinity of jewel-eyed serpents,
In whose patient veins beats the blood slowly,
Men in multitude were beheaded, maidens hurled
From cliffs in propitiation, having knelt first as we now
Over heavenly enigmas suddenly seen in gloom!

Country People Are
Less Alone Than Others

Country people are less alone than others,
Because when living becomes too much to endure
Any more and the burden of infinity presses,
They turn to the animals who are always there.

The sweet-breathed ponderous silken-hided cows
Stand in their stalls like monuments of serenity
To young women wounded by quarrel or bereavement
Or conscious suddenly of the lost hope of eternity.

The old ones pushed aside in haste or hate by kin,
Go to speak to amber eyes of growing beasts
And lean upon the shaggy manes and strong-veined necks
Until themselves are vested again with strength.

Children and young men, making pride their religion,
Cannot therefore weep in the sight of day;
Only in the hot dark stall where the animal stands
Can they become assuaged and begin again to pray.

WHEN I stood at the door of our country home at the ending of my fiftieth year, the trees were shaking in the sunlight, the sky was dazzling, and the scream of Agamemnon, our Blue Peacock, was resounding through the high oaks and maples and pines.

I was thinking how once upon a time, especially when I was very young, although it was true too into my forties, I was religious in that I had a strong feeling that I dealt with some powerful supernatural being. But in my fiftieth year we traveled around the globe, my first journey of the kind, without hotel reservations or a set schedule, seldom knowing which country we would visit next. I observed the customs as well as the beautiful, bizarre, and even fearful ways of worship that were taking place and had taken place over the ages. There was no accompanying shadow then of Barney's or my eventual or imminent death. As the planes took off and landed, I held Barney's hand firmly, and as we touched ground at the end of the trip, I told him, "I know without doubt now that the world is truly round. Also I have become, like you, a believer only in nature. But I will remain superstitious, continuing to knock on wood, cross streets to give money to beggars, speak in a hushed voice of good fortune, and hold your hand when I feel it is necessary."

The trees outside continued to glow, and I thought how there would be no past and no future again after my fiftieth year—only the present and its reality.

MY 50ᵀᴴ YEAR

Around the World Ballad

Her shoes wore out in Kenya
And the Serengeti plain,
Her stockings tore in Thailand
And were never worn again;

She lost her bra in Bali,
And her slip in Singapore,
Her panties fell in Fiji
On Suva's sunny shore;

She came to Easter Island
With a Polynesian air,
Wearing just a muumuu
And a flower in her hair!

Around the World Ballad

Taking the Time

Taking the time in this my fiftieth year
To make my way with husband slowly about the sphere,
Going east and noting among other things
How I have lived for forty-nine winters and fifty-one springs,
For now in November about the equator
Hibiscus and Bougainvillea blossoms are everywhere,
Surviving even dusty ambitious Singapore
And thriving in Bali and the Barrier Reef's green shore,
Fiji and Tahiti and Quito, Ecuador,
Brought by a native porter to my birthday's door.

Taking the time to view myself in a mirror,
Counting the scars mostly vaguely seen,
One winding pink, denoting a Caesarean,
Death skirted and a twenty-seven-year-old son;
A white line on the leg where a sickle swung
And on the hand where my collie's teeth clung,
Forty years past but not forgotten;
Myself now burned brown by the same sun
Which poured violent on Grecian sand,
On works of Egypt's kings and the Serengeti plain
And Easter Island's stone giant men.

Taking the time in this my fiftieth year
To number among others a vigorous mother,
Daughter, son, infant grandson,
Various step-children and their children,
And first among all, loved husband;

Having walked by Tanzania's Masai tribesmen,
Singhalese sari-clad golden women,
Bombay's pavement-sleeping slim Indians,
Blue-black aboriginals of Darwin,
Wild-haired kindly tall Fijians,
And everywhere the slant-eyed helpful Chinamen,
Rounding the globe, noting my fellowmen.

Taking the time to list those lost to me,
Grandmothers, grandfathers, father but lately,
Aunt, sister, cousin,
Forgetting none, mourning friend and relation;
Having stood in the palace of Knossos, the Minoan,
Gazed at the sunken tombs at Tyre in Lebanon,
Crawled through the pyramid which hid Chephron,
Gone faint at the face of Queen Nefertiti
And five-thousand-year-old dusty sarcophagi
And in Pachacamac, Peru, an ungraved mummy;
All lost in the world now named by me.

Taking the time in this my fiftieth year
To note the voices falling on my ear,
The soft-toned affectionate Roman waiter,
The Cretan villager reciting Homer,
In Istanbul a man-saddled street vendor;
Shouted Swahili from a Kenya land rover,
Noisy Cockney Aussies on Sydney Harbor,
Spanish in Santiago, Incan Quechua in Peru,
Until rounding the planet, the tongue becomes at last my own
And is used now by husband, "Helga, we are home."

Treetops

*(Treetops is perched forty feet high, in the branches of a
giant Cape Chestnut tree overlooking a waterhole and salt
lick in the Aberdare National Park in Kenya, East Africa.)*

We had just come from the pyramids, which stood there,
The Sphinx at their feet, on Giza's sands,
Speckled with troops of tourists, souvenir vendors
And Arabs with their bawling pretty camels;
The tombs were five thousand years old at least.

Ghostly procession! In your limestone monstrous dusty blocks,
Your inner polished slabs of alabaster and pink Aswan granite,
Is part of the mystery of ourselves, our possibility!

Here in Treetops twilight, giant Cape buffalo
Are milling below the balcony, roaring at times;
Warthogs go trotting to and fro in the raised dust;
Waterbuck and bushbuck arrive and depart.
Fifty baboons appeared earlier for tea,
Grasping buns and cakes greedily.
At dinner someone said, "A Black Rhino is at the pool!"
And there it was, bent, prehensile-lipped, among the buffalo.
Later in the dark in the floodlights' dim glow
Suddenly someone called, "See, the elephants come!"
Out of the forest, a line of them, as in a dream, scarcely seen.

Ghostly procession! In your dusty monstrous vague forms,
Your ponderous legs and swaying trunks and tails,
Is a part of ourselves; your blood is in our veins,
Our shared ancestor is in our common genes.
The leader turns to face us screaming shrilly
And then drops his trunk to drink deliberately.
His feet together, wide ears fanning out,
Make him a swaying pyramid reversed.
O monumental! Dimly seen, revered, gray-dusted, alive!

On Learning That I May Be About to Die

Surprised while going fast through my middle years
By news: "Of all the tumors you could have had
At least you picked a favorable kind."
"All I want," I said, "is the square and honest truth,"
And went home and put champagne on ice
And had a tray of tea brought up to our bed,
Ranging my dolls and toys before me in a row.
"There is a disease, my dears," I said,
"Which humans, not you, share—eventual death."

Later putting on the long flowered flowing dress
And the opal ring and your golden family chain
And a fresh perfume; combing my hair
And going to set out caviar, waiting your usual coming,
Your cheek cold and snow on your shoulders,
Your eyes delighted, your hands popping the cork,
Pouring the champagne, toasting independence.
Late in the night thinking how I really did not mind
Dying sooner or later and how nothing at all had changed.

Through the Woods Weeping

Through the woods weeping, we walked,
Weeping through the woods and talked continually
On that Wednesday when they said that the cancer had spread,
The lung now involved also and heaven only knew what else
And it was traced there upon the X-ray—round disc-like shadows,
You, a surgeon, knowing the mortal meaning and telling it,
"Else," weeping, "you'll never trust me again."

Feeling the weakening fire streaking through—the sentence,
And leading you to a tree stump and sitting close beside,
"Say now truly, not how long but the shortest time I might have."
"Perhaps six months. But I do not believe in shadows
And the case is too bizarre." "Take a young wife. Promise me this!"
"No. I do not like young women. Only you."
Walking through the woods again, weeping and speaking.

"We will cheat fate," I said, "all life to me is time spent with you.
Come home oftener. And when I die it will be as if I'd lived longer."
"Yes. But why not me? I'm old and I've done everything I ever wanted!"
"It doesn't matter. Love is the only thing."
And spring began to be about us that Wednesday
And the green evening started moving toward darkness
As we went walking through the woods talking until spent and content.

Now That the Fire Is Gone

Now that the fire is gone or can be argued down,
Lying beside you in the bed of our country place
In the dawn of the morning of the operation,
Listening to the waking of April's gray woods outside,
Wild geese screaming and falling into the dark pond below
(On a lake beyond, one lies like a log on her island over eggs),
The rooster crows; soon he will lead his six hens out onto the grass,
The quacking of mallards, the squeaking of wood ducks,
And the movement of my dog as he comes to stand beside my hand.

In the night the fire had risen once, on waking, and I had downed it,
Listening to your deep breathing in the moonlight,
Facing myself becoming a memory (not later but now),
Myself turning into a photograph, "This is how she was. You can see."
The linens in the closets disarrayed, the furniture rearranged
(A ghost, polite, I would say nothing).
Brown petals of a flower falling from a book
And no one knowing from whom they came or why placed there.
Standing at our tableside where the wine glistened
And the silver shone and the noisy arguments were flung about
(Unable to protest and enter in, being slowly erased from the scene,
Becoming a hasty flicker in the house's mirrors, uneasy of discovery
And ever so slowly withdrawing from the living).
The fire subsiding in your slow breathing in and out below the moon.

Now in the dawn, awake with you and ready, packing the bag, fasting,
"Put in a bottle of Scotch and the Yugoslav wine you like,"
You said from the breakfast table. We were pleased with the morning
And I pulled all the gardenia blooms for the plant's sake
And dropped them among the dress and slippers and toothbrush.
Then driving into the city as the sun climbed golden into the day.

Waking in the Dark Land of the Dream

Waking in the dark land of the dream where to and fro
Float, wearing white from cap to shoe, bodiless angels
Whispering, "What can I do for you to make you comfortable?"
"Roll the bed higher. A little lower. The pillow. Oh."
My daughter's face glowing, "Have you heard? You're all right."
"I know." Vaguely remembering you standing above in the dream,
Calling, "The radiation killed the tumor and we'll see about the other."
"I'd like some ice water." "There's a glass on each side of you!"
"The pain." "I'll get something for it right away!" The angel
Flying off and wafting back, the small prickling,
And then the slow overcoming by the power of the morphine
Of all discomfort and replacing it with nothingness.
Over the days, flowers coming and banking windows and tables
And making the land's boundaries, the gardens of the dream,
Familiar faces appearing and disappearing and being unremembered,
And then yours again, laughing, shouting, before being gone,
"Shadows, that was all! A virus or the like. I never believed."
And pulling the sheet up and over myself, shaken,
So the angel breathed, "What's wrong with her?"
And my daughter, "Nothing. That's why she's doing that."
Moving quietly again into the pattern of the pain of the dark land,
Where always within reach of a sigh the white disinvolved angels float,
Breathing their eternal question, "Can I do something for you?"

And Then Going Home Delicately

And then going home delicately so that the belly would hold
And not fall apart as I thought surely it would if given cause,
Easing up the stairway, sliding into our soft bed, alive,
The pink sheets and pillows patterned with roses climbing over roses,
Replacing the high white hard electric one ;
The hospital gowns no more, their strings undone and cast aside,
Wearing only lacy shifts and negligees, satin and brilliant and new ;
The aseptic scents dismissed for my own sweet familiar perfume.

Asking for my dolls and toys again to be brought before me
To show them the new one you gave in celebration,
Tall and mystic and inward glowing, of Lalique crystal,
To tell them once more of that disease that humans share, not they,
And how dying sooner or later still made no difference,
But that I was changed ; *nothing again would ever be the same.*

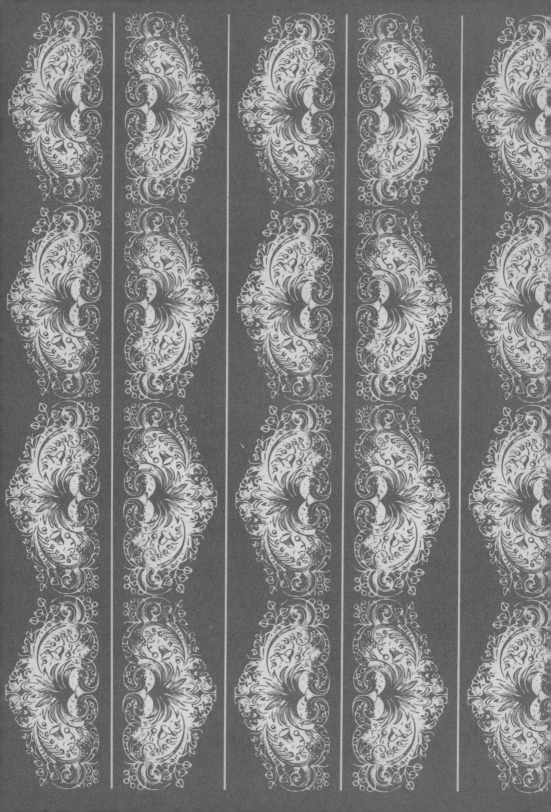